Welcome Distractions

Accessible Poems for Time-Strapped Humans

Carol Wierzbicki

UNBEARABLE BOOKS / AUTONOMEDIA

Series Editors: Jim Feast and Ron Kolm

UB—1: *Spermatagonia: The Isle of Man,* bart plantenga
UB—2: *Negativeland,* Doug Nufer
UB—3: *Neo Phobe,* Jim Feast with Ron Kolm
UB—4: *Shorts Are Wrong,* Mike Topp
UB—5: *The Hotel of Irrevocable Acts,* Carl Watson
UB—6: *The Ass's Tale,* John Farris
UB—7: *This Young Girl Passing,* Donald Breckenridge
UB—8: *Love Does Not Make Me Gentle or Kind,* Chavisa Woods
UB—9: *A Superintendent's Eyes,* Steve Dalachinsky
UB—10: *Kali's Day,* Bonny Finberg
UB—11: *The Rat Hunt Boys,* Anna Mockler
UB—12: *The Beer Mystic,* bart plantenga
UB—13: *Night Shift,* Ron Kolm
UB — 14: *Pareidolia,* Carl Watson
UB — 15: *Long Day, Counting Tomorrow,*
Jim Feast with Carol Wierzbicki
UB—16: *Flasher,* Tsaurah Litzky
UB—17: *Welcome Distractions,* Carol Wierzbicki

ALSO BY CAROL WIERZBICKI

Top Teen Greatest Hits (Poets Wear Prada, 2009 and 2017)

WELCOME DISTRACTIONS

ACCESSIBLE POEMS FOR TIME-STRAPPED HUMANS

CAROL WIERZBICKI

AUTONOMEDIA

ACKNOWLEDGEMENTS

"Philosophy of Lingerie" appeared in *Big Cigars*.
"Listening to Sonny Rollins" appeared in *The Otter*.
"Ode to Brooklyn" appeared in *October Babies*.
"Boot Eating Scooter Trash" appeared in *Pink Pages*.

Unbearable Books are published and distributed by

Autonomedia
POB 568 Williamsburgh Station
Brooklyn NY 11211–0568 USA

www.autonomedia.org
info@autonomedia.org

CONTENTS

POLITICAL, RESIDENTIAL, COMMERCIAL

RELATIONSHIPS

WORDS AND MUSIC

With Thanks to Jim Feast

POLITICAL, RESIDENTIAL, COMMERCIAL

Champion Cat Breeder

So you're big in the poetry world.
Who cares?
It's like being a champion cat breeder
You move in weird, fussy
little circles
where egos erupt like
cat-spit.
Big in the poetry world—
What does that mean?
Do people flock to your side,
hang on your every word?
Well, they're just other poets, aren't they—
they already know what you're going to say
being part of your incestuous
cat-fanciers circle
and they make sure to stroke you
admiringly
as you proudly display the
nose, tail and coat
of your poem,
and laugh at your
lame jokes so you'll publish
their stuff in your
cat-fanciers magazine.
Over the years
the other cat fanciers in your circle
have developed nervous tics:
their ears twitch or
they're always cleaning

some imaginary schmutz
off their whiskers.
If refreshments are offered
they pounce.
Later, they exchange
carefully-worded critiques
between preenings
and gingerly pick their way
among the knots of obscure people
they've resolved to avoid
on their way to kitchen
or litter box.

Editing

This I feel confident
enough to do for free.
I'll be happy to do it for you
as a favor because
I enjoy it,
it comes effortlessly.
Like an expert witness
I don't get paid.
Well, maybe they do get paid but
in — what? — fingernail clippings
and blood?
I'm witness to the horrors of the
first draft, all
the embarrassing things
the writer would wish
had never seen the light of day
if he or she could view it through
my eyes.

There's a lot of dust floating around
my apartment
but at my editing job
(the one I do get paid for)
I breathe filtered air;
it's really more of an umbilical cord
than a job.

My favorite pens now
are erasable.

The Theme Is Civic Pride

Write a poem about your neighborhood
for the patriotism contest
while the hope inside you
flickers like the light
in your project building's elevator

Write this poem about your neighborhood —
whose four walls you are in danger of looking at
for the rest of your life —
and buy your way out
with your words.

Describe a beautiful scene
outside your window
even if that scene is confined to
a drop of dew
on a blade of grass
poking through the sidewalk.
Your neighborhood isn't going anywhere,
but you are, for better or worse.

Write an essay,
gifted child,
and know the loneliness of transcendence.
There's no return ticket on this train.

Your friends run around, around the bases
while you in the library
turn pages forward, forward,

like a marathon runner
never looking back.

Write a poem about your neighborhood
because the judges of the contest,
dangling the carrot of
scholarship, grant, gift,
are looking for an authentic homeboy
to co-opt. It's up to you to decide
whether or not you're for sale.

Beyoncé at the Super Bowl

There she is
in her Xena Warrior Princess outfit —
leather but with strategic lace inserts at the thigh —
she's tough, but tender — it's a paradox!

Hundreds of clones of her
flash across an infinite chain of Jumbotrons,
smoke machines and simulated fire threaten to engulf the stage;
torches shoot 50 feet in the air.
Air from unseen propellers fans her hair
so that it blows just right — *Vogue*-cover perfect!

Hundreds of leather-clad beauties
prance in time — her New Model Army!
(But… what are they fighting?!)

Halftime ends. Play resumes.
Testosterone replaces the
estrogen extravaganza we've just witnessed.

Then, with no 2-minute warning: BLACKOUT!
Half the stadium goes dark.
It's just like the Brooklyn Bridge after
Hurricane Sandy:
Brooklyn side lit, Manhattan dark.
For 34 minutes, idling players
and uneasy broadcast patter take over:
"Warn me next time you recharge your phone, Bob, heh, heh…"
Is anyone in the crowd thinking about that *other* stadium
years ago, ceiling imploding from Katrina?

Finally the refs take the field once more and everyone cheers,
forgetting the lights went out for America
in more ways than one.

9/11 Paradox

The towers fall and Mary Tyler Moore tosses her beret into the air.
Fun-seeking East Villagers enjoy the late autumn day courtesy
    of global warming.
Schooled illiteracy composes advertising billboards. Arrogance
is what makes a rock 'n roll song work.
Political boosters dole out hanging chads on Election Day.
Inertia drives the working masses.
Exclusivity is the real community-builder.
World peace threatens homeland security.
The internet is a Tower of Babel.
Planes crashing into skyscrapers are the ultimate push media—
we cannot look away.

Ode to Brooklyn

You, with your trash-strewn corners,
your tacky little mom-and-pop shops,
your slovenly ways, your foul-mouthed denizens,
rambling fences and
stoops lifting grandiloquently into the air
dreaming of Parthenon greatness
extravagantly neglected parks, a chance for
crabgrass to grow, mongrel dogs and cats to couple,
horns to honk, birds to flip.

You, with your rusting smokestacks,
your vigilante block associations,
chain-smoking beauty salon owners and patrons,
over-the-top Christmas displays crowding your
postage stamp-sized front lawns,
marketing slogans that breed like flies
your brass-knuckle childhoods,
your forsythia stubbornly flourishing
beside the grimiest warehouses,
your incongruously ultramodern gas stations,
your overpasses and viaducts,
a thousand negative spaces for neighborhood kids
to unfurl their evil games,
lawnmowers, awnings your thwarted attempts
at upscale suburbia.

Your beat cops,
your wastrel saints,
your shaving cream Halloweens,

your makeshift patios and barbecue pits,
your greetings delivered like a threat
— Howthehellareya? —
your Saturday revels, your Sunday grudges,
brick the color of dried blood,
sentiments exposed like scabs
as summertime debates heat
stoop and street.

Because you are forever a work in progress, Brooklyn,
your streets under construction,
neighborhoods newly named
like recently reclaimed bastard children,
this poem could go on forever and probably will,
like my commute on this neverending F train.

Blues

Disheartening, how
the Wall-Streeters
incorporate street words
into their lexicon:
Done Deal.

Repeat:
It is not my fault he is on crack.
It is not may fault they are rich.

Poor dopes at Miserly Publishing, Inc.
dress chicly in shades of pitch
for the office:
they think they have careers
like the ones depicted
in Glamour magazine,
or maybe they're just
frustrated club kids
heading our after work
in tight clusters.

Call this day
a done deal:
it is not my fault
the sun is going down.

Age

We're living in a disposable age, a polemical age, a laughable age, a tragical age, a changeable age. An age of individuality that curls back toward conformity like a snake eating its tail. A digital age of tweets and posts and texts and yet an age where we crave face-to-face contact. It's an age of excess and yet not having enough. An age of hate and yet of radical love cradling the hated ones.

It's an age of extreme weather: fires, floods, tornadoes, hurricanes, and intensely beautiful days. An age of jealously guarded privacy and unprecedented surveillance. An age of space travel and deep drilling. Of discovery and discovering how little we actually know. Of unstoppable development and naturally reclaimed land, flowers blooming above sludge.

A paradoxical age of rural lifestyle movements within cities: beehives and tomato plants on rooftops, crops of corn and herbs in parking lots — where we're both locavore and globally connected. An age where the city has no future and IS the future.

Where we all speak different languages and yet push the same buttons.

Cat Exit

The cat exits,
too smart and too quick for us
inferior humans.

The same diversion never works twice
with a cat —
you must change your stratagem
    every time,
or they're on to your game.

The cat exits,
leaps onto the top of the kitchen cupboards,
then jumps down when prodded
with the Swiffer mop,
dashes behind the couch,
now to the counter,
back behind the couch —
it's hopeless!

The cat exits, and at the point
we turn our backs on her
in despair,
she makes a casual beeline
for the jail
we've prepared.

Anti-Revolution

I'm antisocial!
I like curfews and pop quizzes.
I like it dark and quiet.
I like the shortened days
when kids are forced to curtail
their basketball games,
collect their baseball bats and bases,
and head home.

Kids tearing down the sidewalk on their scooters?
Might as well wave a red flag in front of
this bull, it enrages me so.

I want muffled ambition,
corked exuberance,
dampened joy.
I want rain on all parades.

I wince at excited
anticipatory squeals —
they are as nails on a chalkboard
to me.

I'm not a killjoy;
I just want people
to stop telling me to smile.

Luxury Is…

new spring trees
glowing like phosphorescent wigs
under the streetlamps
as I look up at the windows
of the yuppie lofts across the street
from the former stevedores’ flophouse
that is my home

Coin Wars: Sacagawea vs. Susan B. Anthony

On the one hand you have Susan:
severe, sharp-faced woman, in profile;
she looks not at us, trapped as she is
in the depressing 70s economy.

And on the other you have Sacagawea,
posing with her papoose on her back,
her smiling face ready to guide the settlers
to a welcoming place.

One coin is dull silver, the other warm gold.

On Susan B.'s flip side you have an
eagle arrogantly landing on the moon;
it was from our era of space conquests.
He looks warhawk-ish.

On Sacagawea's flip side you have that
same eagle, but he's soaring, not landing,
and not placed
in any context but the air.

When I hand my Sacagawea coin to the Ecuadoran
lady in the women's locker room
to rent a towel,
she beams her approval:
"Gold. Nice."

When I use the Susan B.,
people think it's a quarter
and return her hostile glare.

Top 10 Ways to Get into the Next Whitney Biennial
(with apologies to David Letterman)

10. Find your old diary from junior high school and scribble on each page with a red magic marker

9. Duct-tape your blowdryer to a piece of drywall

8. Find 10,000 "backspace" keys and make a mosaic. Title it "Productivity" or "Bill Gates in Shangri-La"

7. Place a baby elephant in a dumpster. Explain that it is interactive video from Poland

6. Take a cheesecake shot of your mother with no bra wearing a T-shirt that says, "I'm Downloadable!"

5. Make a multimedia piece that's so complicated no one (even you) can access the site

4 Put the Pope's holographic image on a credit card

3. Set up an answering machine that plays "Hi! I can't come to the phone right now" on a continuous loop

2. Feed your dog some peanut butter. Let the camera roll until he's finished licking it all off

1. Write an Oscar acceptance speech for the recipient of the "best key grip" award

Avon

As I played with my mother`s
Avon perfume bottles,
each label seemed to promise
the fulfillment of a different
aspect of womanhood:
Occur! with its swirling, breathless script
suggesting undreamed-of litheness;
Roses, Roses' melancholy
assuring a graceful, elegant old age;
Field Flowers light and girlish.

I'd unscrew the plastic top —
a trompe l'oeil lilac bouquet —
trying to get a whiff of my future:
would I be Marlo Thomas in "That Girl"
swinging a parasol?
Gidget? Samantha Stevens?
That breezy Jeannie in a bottle?

Like the aroma of the petrified
Her Prettiness cream sachet
unused and then discarded,
those pastel figments
faded.

12th Anniversary of 9/11

Written 9/11/13

I'll tell you something good that happened after 9/11: it left an empty space, and silence, if only for a day. When the 9/11 anniversary rolls around, when the great cosmic calendar flips yet again to the date that's indelibly etched in all our minds, I take it as a cue (or excuse) to pause, slow down, halt the trajectory of my rushing from meaningless errand to pointless job, and ponder chaos and what that really is.

Is chaos the routine, the daily grind, in which we ignore or suppress our most ardent desires, hopes and dreams? Or is it the occasional imposition of disaster that signifies a world spinning out of control? I'd watched the whole thing unfold on TV all those years ago, everything in me numb but my eyeballs, which were saturated with images of fire, collapse — but mostly talking heads blabbering nonsense. My eyes burned, were scratchy from absorbing so much media smoke and mirrors.

9/11 is a handy reminder that the halls of power can be blown away as dust, and that human bone and blood and tissue can commingle with what was once an architect's dream. The unthinkable can happen, and it can be awful, or grand, or both.

I like the photos I saw in today's *New York Times*, especially a closeup of hands tenderly tracing one of the names etched in the memorial railing, and one of a mother praying with her young son at the edge, her brow furrowed in concentration, their faces shadowed by grief yet pondering the infinite lying at the bottom of the abyss, trying to make sense of it all. I like these photos of softened humanity, quiet heads bowed, not pursuing anything. They appear as under a veil, a veil of bruised grace.

At my church's 9/11 service, I wear a scarf that looks like smoke. I meditate on the atomization of the routine, as particles of souls inch toward the sky.

To David Villalobos

You wanted to be
"one with the tiger."
What was it about the image of him
burned so brightly for you?

It was a hair-trigger decision,
jumping off that sterile monorail
and into the heart of darkness.

Bachuta, the striped Siberian beauty,
played the gracious host
by not snapping your jugular.

Now you lie in your hospital bed,
all broken bones and gashes,
listlessly checking your Facebook page
where the week before you'd posted
"Mother Earth is my religion."
Now you're the butt of everyone's jokes.

But it was a leap of faith,
this desire to transcend that urban preserve
and become prey.

Rest, rest, one whose name means
"House of Wolves" —
quiet the howling in your head
and dream of
a bestial communion without barriers.

Look out your window.
See how the stars come out
and the moon blesses your wounds.

The Hard Way

(inspired by "Crazy Dog Events,"
from Jerome Rothenberg's *Shaking the Pumpkin*)

I want to marry a Michigan militia-man who craves the taste of blood
I want to bring back 70s hairstyles
I want to reinvent prayer
I want to taunt muggers
I want to pickle my liver slowly, over time,
with little sips of scotch from a hidden flask
I want to order every single item from the J. Peterman catalog,
one each day, and pay the shipping charges
I want to make tortillas from scratch
I want to walk to work from Bay Ridge,
even though I don't live in Bay Ridge
I want to make tea from tealeaves grown in my backyard
I want to sleep on the roof year-round
I want to call up the man I haven't spoken to in two years
and ask, "What's happening with our relationship?"
I want to eat ice cream with my hands and soup with chopsticks
I want to have sex in the church confessional, confessing all the while
I want to send back the wine at Bouley
I want to vote for every candidate in the party marked "Other"
I want to write long poems on sugar packets
I want to swim like Flipper with Newt Gingrich on my back
I want to keep calling the number with the busy signal
I want to attempt a double axel with my flabby thighs
I want to sip from the water's edge
I want to rewrite the Bible as a Buddhist tract
I want to meticulously record the ravings of schizophrenics
I want to leave the entire Kama Sutra on my answering machine

I want to piece together a quilt of postage stamps
I want to petition all the office buildings to play Kurt Weill
   in their elevators and lobbies
I want to take Flamenco lessons from a snobby and
   temperamental choreographer
I want to use my pinkie as a unit of measure to calculate the volume
   of a cloud
I want to hitch my Pinto station wagon to a star
I want to write my term paper in the most intricate calligraphy
I want to raise my child to take risks
I want to dance on the head of a pin in high heels
I want to take my driver's test blindfolded
I want to have Tourette's Syndrome around guys I'm attracted to
I want to catch snowflakes on my tongue in Times Square
   while crossing against the light
I want to take the Stairmaster to heaven

Office Dress Code

What is the office dress code today?
it's as capricious as the Dragon Lady's moods;
only jeans are forbidden.
"Are those jeans, Carol?" she barks.

Today I am
a little old Cuban man:
striped trousers, straw fedora,
man's knit short-sleeve pullover with French seaming.
(All I need is a cigar.)

Another day,
I'm Frida Kahlo,
dripping with religious icons:
crosses, heavy wooden rosary beads.

One day, I'm wearing
thrift-store men's wool houndstooth blazer
with cryptic pins on the lapel:
tiny gold hammer from Habitat for Humanity,
military-looking pin from Watford Lawn Bowling Association,
my immigrant grandmother's Victory pin from working at
the Packard auto plant in Detroit during WWII.
I'm paying tribute to her Rosie-the-Riveter
can-do spirit.
But the Dragon Lady frowns at them, perturbed:
these little anomalies scramble
her Fashion Police radar.

Or I'm Sophia Loren
in 1956 Rome,
black cotton *strega nonna* shirtwaist dress
with sly eyelet inserts
worn without a slip of course!
mounting my rusty bicycle
to go buy a loaf of bread.

Another day, another costume:
Annie Hall in baggy pants,
gypsy in swirling full skirt
depicting scenes of a Moroccan bazaar
I will never visit.

Unincorporated Township

An aborted city
with half a brain
too small to be counted as a
Standard Metropolitan Statistical Area
with trees the size of thumbnails
and kids who never close their mouths
riding battered skateboards
with pitted metal wheels

An open septic tank
its voters unregistered
its population sliding smoothly under the census
your dustbowl cousins live here
as does the half-brother you've managed to forget
the heads of households have jobs
that constantly take them
on the road, leaving families perpetually
missing a limb
and at night when their dependents fall asleep
it's to the white noise of
indifferent trucks rolling by
on their way to someplace with solid borders

The town hall stands unfinished
over earth that is brown and cracked
to match the radon-soaked brick
of the hastily knocked-up dwellings

The snow that falls here
turns beige on contact
and the people that die here
do so in midsentence

My Apology to Saks 5th Ave.

I'm sorry!
I tend to wear things until they become old and soft, misshapen;
I grow attached to things,
so I don't shop often at stores like yours.

I don't deserve to be here
I feel out of place
wandering among your white walls
and shiny black shelves
and unforgiving light
and angular salespeople.

What must I do to become worthy?
Lose weight? Find a job in a higher tax bracket?
Though I really do have more than enough,
walking your floors
full of unrelatable clothes,
I feel paradoxically deprived.

Oh, Saks 5th Ave.,
here I am, playing at being a privileged white woman —
I *am* a privileged white woman!
My guilt at being here cuts both ways:
I don't earn enough money to shop here,
but I can still browse the sale racks
in comfortable anonymity;
no security personnel
will suddenly appear alongside me,
grabbing my thin, lily-white wrist.

I'm sorry!
I'm not a responsible shopper.
It's been so long I've forgotten
how to behave in a place like this.
I get so easily lost
(and I know your store is laid out this way on purpose),
my meanderings so circular
I inevitably need a Ladies Room
(which you so discreetly label "Ladies Lounge").
Yes, "Ladies Lounge" —
that's how I know I'm in a place I can't afford!
Half my apartment could fit inside
your "Ladies Lounge,"
and oh, the desperation there:
the stalls just dirty enough
to remind you you're still in New York,
the chips in the marble on the counters and sinks,
the non-working soap dispenser or faucet
I always seem to pick,
and the empty cashier stations.
It's like a Twilight Zone episode
where a bomb has wiped out the earth's entire
population
except for (oh bitter irony) one person — me!
the alien shopper
who never belonged.

Demographic

I think I'll have a Black weekend
sip Colt 45
dream of Billy Dee Williams
handing me smooth lines
listen to rap
line some fatcat's pockets with
my futile pursuit of
house/car/stereo
while I chew
the Mickee-Dee of forgetfulness
and yes I do want fries with that

Because you see
it's not just a Black weekend
it's my weekend too
encouraging me to go out and spend
too much money: the soul arrangement
of the beer jingle
soaring to Gospel heights
instead of blue-eyed rock 'n roll
a bull or a lion on the label
in place of a Gothic crest

I think I'll be Black this weekend
try to recreate tableaus
of elegant folks in evening gowns
and pimp costumes
spread out on polar bear rugs
before a crackling fire

and find primitive tribal bliss
in my fifth floor walkup
safe and warm in the strategically programmed embrace
of the TV's blue light

I think I'll have a women's weekend
yes be a modern woman
who can water ski
and even slalom
with her tampon
firmly in place
I'll be a modern woman this weekend
never come home tired or irritable
but cheerfully care for
my husband and children
even with a wracking, miserable
cold
I think I'll have a women's weekend
stroll in a wheatfield
clothed in white
my scarves trailing behind me
in slow motion
be hauntingly beautiful
even if I'm just the
waitress behind the counter
serving greasy fries
or mom
trying to get a grass stain
out of Billy's shorts

Or I'll be an active senior
roaming the beach with my
Irish Setter
in a fisherman's sweater
sit out that hurricane
like the grizzled old-timer I am

Or a house pet:
meow and bark on cue
retrieve a thousand Frisbees
look elegant and regal
on velvet cushions
practice my adoring look
knock the receiver cunningly
off its cradle and demand
the preferred brand
I think I'll be a house pet this weekend
save an infant from a fire
paddle gallantly in the family pool
stick my paw into the goldfish bowl

for you see
stereotype is commodity
the commercials won't let you
just be
your life is theirs
and this limited-time introductory offer
is free

Thunderstorm

I can hear Slim Pickens, riding
toward the millennium on his
bucking bronco bomb.
I can hear them screaming down in
Times Square for the Backstreet Boys.
I can't see the tip of the Chrysler Building
through the fog
but I can imagine
the New Year's ball dropping
on Chinese gymnast Sang Lan's foot.
Here in my almost-corner office
I enjoy a commanding view
of pre-apocalyptic Gotham skyline
while the Chrysler does her
dance of the seven veils.
As the famous high-school student
gunman once said: peekaboo!
Someone emailed me
asking if I was hiding under my
desk with grounding wires in my hands
to avoid being hit by the lightning.
Actually that advice makes a lot
of sense.
There's nothing to do today
but wait… wait…
Wait. I think I hear Slim now:
Eeeeee-hoooo!
Eeeeee-hoooo!

My Epitaph

I will die
at the fork of a snowy brook
crouched between splayed legs
of rushing water.

Dreaming of Goa

With thin brown fingers
smelling of curry
the woman removes the hair
from my upper lip
using a thread twisted
and stretched taut
between her clenched teeth.
With her back to the snow
falling outside the shop window,
she is dreaming of a beach
in Goa,
and colors that are
impossible now.

Spring Thaw

I like the idea of a watch
  driven by a heartbeat,
and clocks fueled by the sun,
and a job touched by luck.
The earth's rotation propelled
by a cat's introspective purr
as a warming trend
quickens the universe.

Carriage horses stamp and snort
 under the blood moon,
and rabbits nibble the leaves
 in the vineyard:
a midnight tableau
of peaceful cohabitation.

The breath of a penitent
 melts frost into dew —
in other words,
spring arrives.

The tributaries of the creek
  travel in all directions,
coaxed by snowmelt.

There is ample flour and sugar
in the larder,
sifted from the wings
 of woodland fairies.

There are no velvet ropes on the world,
  no locked doors,
and as luck would have it,
you're on the VIP list,
and so is everyone else.

Letter to a Security Guard

August 1996
Linthicum (outside Baltimore)

You sit your lonely paunch down on the "park" bench as I amble by. I used to work at a godforsaken armored outpost like yours, vast parking lots next to mid-sized office buildings, where the impeccably landscaped grounds were never meant to be enjoyed on a walk and the strictly cosmetic benches were never meant to be used for more than an hour at a time, for hyper-accelerated lunches, for tightly scheduled, convulsive rendezvous.

I worked at an ad agency in a suburb of Detroit, in a corporate library that kissed the butt of advertising that in turn had its lips firmly planted on the rear of the auto and airline industries. At lunch I found places to walk, though I felt discouraged in my endeavor at every step, with every intrusive curb and truncated sidewalk. Though the concept of outdoor public spaces did not exist there, I persevered, grinding out my hate for my job and my yearning for a recently departed friend (he had hightailed it to New York) as I pushed back, back beyond the arena-sized parking lot, beyond the stunted trees of the median strips, and ultimately to the blasted heath of the residential subdivision that rose in the distance like some oasis for the dead. One hour to haul my AWOL fugitive butt past the purring cars of noontime, the occasional purposeful clicking of Avon lady pumps, the unanimously shuttered and drowsing homes. We all abstain, they seemed to say.

I wonder what it is you're thinking as I walk past. I have no business at your building — I'm staying at the hotel one desolation over, traveling for my job, the mission being to learn a useless computer desktop publishing package so malevolently baroque that it's guaranteed to make by job a living hell. I'm just rambling until the trail runs out. I've seen the back of my hotel, and like all the backsides of hotels everywhere it makes me want to go out and shoot myself, having as it does all the requisite components of desperation: few pre-dinner kids at the pool, menacing exhaust fans, dumpsters, and disenfranchised franchise service personnel all in white, standing around smoking outside the servants' entrance.

Back in Michigan at the ad agency, I guarded useless — or maybe I should say disused — property, just like you. Though I was working in a corporate reference library, no one ever seemed to know how to look something up in a book. I watched the ants enter and leave the sugar bowl, sometimes with their prizes firmly clamped in their mandibles. As Bill Clinton would say, I feel your pain.

Or rather your emptiness. My feet crunched in rust-belt gravel as I thought of everyone looking forward to heading out for Ladies Nite after work at one of those local bars whose bleach-y disinfectant odor slaps you in the face the moment you enter. The signs and blinking lights screaming, "Have fun!" while the smell growls, "Sterilize." Lite FM radio spots for said bar played over and over in my head as I walked, working me up into an impotent rage.

The trail has run out, so I double back. I alight on the same park bench I saw you sitting on, and I'm wondering (though it's getting late and you're long gone, the parking lot starting to thin out) whether you weren't being a bit rebellious by stepping outdoors for a few minutes to escape the stale recycled white-collar service-sector air, whether you were acting out of defiance as your feet crunched through gravel, or whether you just fancied a smoke.

Must end this letter. I'm not supposed to be here; the compound keeps trying to spit me out. I'm an unwelcome biological form, foreign blip on the radar of the uninhabitable. I feel prying eyes behind the glass, imagine you peering, perplexed, from your podium as I pause in the middle of this afterthought sidewalk to write these last observations. My field glasses look into my soul and yours, and as I listen to the birds in the encroached woods begin their evening song, I think I can almost hear, behind their soft, tentative whispers, the outraged cries of the tallied, the market-segmented, the subdivided.

Mammogram

We're sitting here in our blue paper gowns
like wallflowers at a dance.
Our wrist corsages are
coiled telephone cords with keys to lockers containing
our civilian clothes.
Lined up against the wall, it's like we're
waiting to have our pictures taken.
There is no Homecoming King,
only the angel of death lurking inside
the X-ray machine.

Stargazing

Rumors of a meteor shower.
We choose grandmother's backyard
because the plants that grow there
with wild abandon
form a natural barrier against
what astronomers refer to as
"light pollution"
from streetlamps, billboards, traffic.
I watch my brother silently
adjust the eyepiece.
We wait.
The sentinel telescope turns
with the turning sky
like a security camera.
Now he's attaching a camera
with a special setting for night.

The perplexed look
on the cat's face the final blooming, fuzzy galaxy
before daybreak.

RELATIONSHIPS
(BEFORE CELL PHONES & SOCIAL MEDIA)

Philosophy of Lingerie

Why the flaming red satin?
Why not emerald green
or royal blue or
screaming yellow,
  for that matter?

No.
Lingerie should be
the color of the
earth's juices,
  grass-green,
  worn, eroded
  root-white,
  bald brown

and should speak
softly of bondage,
should be trimmed
with rope,
frayed at the shoulders,
loose ends of string unraveling
at the neck
and wrists.

There is nothing romantic
or even slightly suggestive
about perky, starched
and overbleached
white lace
springing enthusiastically
to the touch;

wear rather
old lace on your nuptial
worried through with holes,
torn and dripping,
revealing surprising,
asymmetrical patches
of body…and psyche.

No crisp eyelet:
swaddle your quickened
heartbeat
in 30's black chiffon
and old shoes
that squeak
when you walk.

No satin ribbons:
tie your corset
with old shoelaces
from your childhood,
from your ears hang
shipwrecked heirlooms,
fasten bras with
creased photographs.

Let the torn hem
stray from your foot as you walk,
increasing the yearning,
stretching out the darkness.

Things I Need at the Store

Why
do I ask
if you and she are "serious"?
No reason really.
Well, plenty of them, actually.
But I am so tired of
telling men how I feel
so they can hurt me
more efficiently.

I'll just say
I would like you back
in my life in some capacity.
The pointy head of this poem
is due to the fact that I'm writing it
on a pad of paper with
"Things I Need at the Store"
printed at the top
and a picture of
a milk carton
a loaf of bread
and a stick of butter
and
"Eastern Paralyzed Veterans Association"
printed across the bottom.
Why
is it I
can never find the right piece
of paper on which
to list the things I need most?

Love Poem

"Come to bed" you said,
pressing my hips suggestively.
"Follow me."
I was tired and hungry:
"But I've got beans
cooking on the stove."
"Beans can be reheated," you said.

I would like to rewrite
the ending to this poem
and take your hand.

Yank (in honor of Lorena Bobbitt)

You flip me over like a pancake
shout my name as if
trying to find me in a crowd
just when I think you're going to
you try the side entrance
  (side? Do you want to create another
   orifice in me?)
pin my limbs out of reach
your shoulder denting my face
my nose to the proverbial
grindstone

We're like dodge 'em cars looking
for an accident
I want chalkmarks on the sidewalk
flashbulb lightning stinging
your face

You shatter over me
but it's I who feel fragmented

We chase after
a ball that we keep throwing
and spitefully kicking
further and further
into traffic
amid the river of indifferent cars
we stare at each other

finally knowing
there is no way back
there is no other side

Cell Phones: Early Observations

So you can be talking
to the object of your desire
even as you approach the place
where he or she is.

In the soft moments in which
you anticipate your reunion,
you can actually be talking
to the person.

It doesn’t seem right.

Tripping

(for my father)

he took a nip in time
with a sudden entropic
hic
cup
transforming kinetic energy
into something deliciously
reversed
for one instant
all strictness and order
turned upside down
doubletime chaos
nothing so hip
as
Dick Van Dyke's flip
over the ottoman
but his deliberate
slip-
up
a betrayal of his latent
, forgiving grace
my world hinged on
unexpected syncopated
sound of footfalls
as he abandoned
himself to a split-second
burst of inspired nihilism:
you'd never know
his favorite work motto was
"presentation is everything"

Repast

I share my overripe pears
with him, and the wine.
His inferior filed-down teeth
chew the fruit with difficulty.
He does not take off his coat.
In the past half hour
he has called me three times
from a pay phone on the street,
deftly shooting holes
in all my positions
with his velvety voice
reminiscent of Tormé.
We sit side by side
on the edge of my bed.
Aching from a love gone bad,
I have suddenly become
a person who would
harbor someone
I am afraid of turning into.
His needs seem simple at first:
he needs a place to flop
but once he's settled in,
starts talking about his crazy
ex-wives.
I'm never quite sure
whether to believe his stories.
Even under his penetrating gaze,
the gentle, questioning burr
in his voice,
I cannot show him
The bruised pear of my heart.

My Romance with You

was a glorious disaster.
How I loved the smashed buildings,
the fires in the streets,
the hoodlums and the barking.

Just as I felt a deep affection for
the ransacking tornado,
the balloon that got away,
and the terrible truth discovered
followed by a moan,
a cry, a
and a faint.

I Am Not an Organic Girl

I overheard some boys in the street and they said,
"These organic girls, I heard they were…"
I didn't hear the rest
as they drifted away in the rain
but I imagine that they
are the kind of girls who
make their own sushi
smell of wheat grass juice
and perhaps went to finishing-school
but like to smoke the rasta guys' ganja weed.

I am not an organic girl
in fact I am very
adulterated.
I do not roll out of bed
in the morning
with no makeup looking gorgeous.

I contain many additives
I'm synthetic and proud
I am not an organic girl
I am highly spiced,
sliced and diced,
and the parties I throw
no one ever hears about
because they're interior journeys.
Not raves — meditation sessions.
But you'll leave levitated
just the same.

Only

(for Hortensia)

If Hortensia
could eat only one kind of food
it would be Japanese:
ascetic miso, decadent sushi.
If she
could have only one toy
it would be click-clacks:
plastic balls on the end of
a wand, tantalizing you to trancelike joy
or shattering in your face.
Her one cosmetic:
nail polish, black and pink.
And if she could take home only
one item from the hardware store
it would be lightbulbs, lightbulbs
by the case,
so she could invite the world in
and see how many of its infinite types —
engineers, Polacks, Surrealists, Sufi —
it would take
to screw one in.

Stitch ’n Bitch

was the name of the sewing class
my fashion designer friend Thea taught
at the gay men’s health center.
“Drive safe”
was her motto
as the boys
carefully guided the fabric
under the foot
of their donated industrial
sewing machines.
Pillows and fabric knapsacks
were turned out,
and leather jackets repaired,
as the boys dished the dirt
about celebrities
and friends alike:
who was taking a trip to Paris,
who was down with a bad cold.

But the need that came up
most often
was the taking in:
cinching the waists
of jeans, the proverbial
tightening of one’s belt
against the inescapable wasting.

I helped where I could,
lending my amateur sewing advice

if Thea was busy.
I got a T-shirt for my meager offering,
never dreaming
that two years later
someone I loved
would be there, summing up his need
in an application.

"Drive Safe"
I can still hear Thea saying
as her boys learned
to take a stitch in time.

Let's Conspire

You bring your smoking gun,
I'll bring my grassy knoll
and we'll rendezvous at the book depository
or any other no-tell place
you deem suitable.
Hold my hand over the burning candle's flame
and I'll leap over your 18-minute gap.
I want to be on someone's blacklist
even if it means we must go underground
for our forbidden heretical trysts.
O shoot out the wind chimes beneath my eaves,
slip a date-rape drug into my Molotov cocktail,
huddle in my bomb shelter.
A little policeman is shining
a flashlight in my head:
let's foment insurrection
in my backseat.

The Hearse for Tsaurah Litzky

The hearse for Tsaurah Litzky is a little red Corvette
The hearse for Tsaurah Litzky knows there exists a chance
  for everything and a technique for nothing
The hearse for Tsaurah Litzky's stereo plays only Ravel, Meat Loaf,
  Janis Joplin and Brazilian torch songs
The hearse for Tsaurah Litzky runs on root vegetables and wet
dreams
The hearse for Tsaurah Litzky needs a hosing down followed by
a hot wax
The hearse for Tsaurah Litzky begs to be taken to the drive-in
  on Saturday night
The hearse for Tsaurah Litzky brakes for women in headscarves,
  teenage parents, and the lonely
The hearse for Tsaurah Litzky is able to miraculously generate a
parking
  space
The hearse for Tsaurah Litzky has a Bronx cheer for a horn
  and mudflaps for despair
The hearse for Tsaurah Litzky ignores the other red Corvettes
  but tails the ice-blue Camaro from Jersey with wire spoke
wheel covers
The hearse for Tsaurah Litzky avoids the Via Venuto
  while it seeks out the obscure medieval side streets
The hearse for Tsaurah Litzky never coasts but has been known
to cruise
The hearse for Tsaurah Litzky has an ample and forgiving back seat
The hearse for Tsaurah Litzky crashes through the police barriers
  of inhibition
The hearse for Tsaurah Litzky has loudspeakers blaring,
  "This town is being officially occupied by Love and Desire"

The hearse for Tsaurah Litzky has drag-races with Destiny
The hearse for Tsaurah Litzky makes hairpin turns
  on bad hair days

Sushi Poem

I want to cut your sushi baby
slice it just right
find the spot of bliss
on bed of salmon pink

I want to cut your sushi
fold it soft 'n silky
roll it in seaweed
blanket it with cool rice

The turquoise counter
the wide steel cutting surface
the platform of my desire
the stage for our love

Ramun, udon, tekka maki
crab, shrimp tempura, teriyaki
ginger pickle, wasabi kiss
our raw-boned love is wrapped in this

Let me hack your fish
let me serve your dish
let me chop your sticks
let me won ton your eel don

I want to bring your nigiri
I want to miso you till you're weary
I'll be your expert samurai
make you beg for my shumai

I'm your master of squid
your emperor of soba
your noodle kamikaze
your buckaroo banzai

I reign over the kingdom
of the raw and the cooked
O roll with me
on our endless seaweed water bed
let's stew in a huge vat of boiling rice
emerge skinless
and mambo like sumo locked
in a sweaty warrior dance

Homestead Bar

(for Ron Kolm)

"You are Anna Karenina"
old man at the Polish bar
says to me, pointing to my
cinched cotton batik dress.
Later, another says to my
friend Sharon
(she's Polish like me):
"I am good comrade, I have
hot shower! You come!"
On the pool table
balls smack and drop
as young stringy boys
in the corner practice
underage drinking.
From cheap vodka tonics
and excellent Polish beer
pour forth debates and laughter;
over our heads the fake
chandelier sheds holy light,
not withholding,
generous and loud
as our fearless leader's laugh.

After Choir Practice

Her face looked windburned. Maybe her psyche was too. She asked us to watch her bags while she left to get something. "You can trust us, we're with a church choir," Jan answered jokingly. We ordered and sat down at the tiny table in the small, cramped health-food take-out joint. Every time someone entered the place, a cold blast of winter air rushed in. But soon our faces were being warmed by giant bowls of beans and rice, soup and pasta. While we ate, the woman returned and ordered her food. As she asked us questions about our food, there seemed to be something a little off about her. When she sat back down at her table, we continued our conversation, paying her little attention. I learned about Jan's parents who lived on a mountain in Pennsylvania, about Tony's Spanish and Italian ancestry, about nude sunbathing in Europe (this from Dorothy), and about Nancy's film on Cuban émigrés. Suddenly I sensed a stillness in the corner of my right eye. I looked over, and the woman was dozing. While I was watching, the cook brought her food, a bowl of broth with beautiful cucumbers and carrots floating in it. She touched her gently on the shoulder to let her know. The woman roused herself briefly, but soon she was once again slumped over the table, oblivious to us, the smells of the food, the winter blasts. I wondered what series of events conspired to bring her to this state, so oblivious was she to the stimulation nearby. I wondered if I would ever get "like that," so lonely that a little joint like this (she had to be a regular) became as familiar as my apartment, where I would doze over my meal as if it were on a TV tray on my bed.

Short-Eared Owls

(for my father-in-law, Paul)

We take the pickup to the middle of the preserve,
and wait.
Evening falls slowly.
Then out of nowhere
the short-eared owls
bloom at the ends of stalks
like milkweed glowing in the dusk,
searching for nocturnal prey.

Paul was father, mate, teacher,
stern expression from a life
of war and academic rigor —
but with a hair-trigger wit
that flashed subtly
as the beat of a raptor's wing.

Imperfect Love Donut

(for John)

I'm sitting here at the Twin Donut, my favorite atmosphere-less place for strangling my hopes and ambitions dead. Your ghost is here, in each disinfected corner. We had breakfast here after what remains the most decadent night of my life, and I relive that night and morning in every hurry-sloshed cup of coffee, every bleached plate, every hard, unyielding curve of the Formica, every overheard dismal encounter.

After our confused black and red night, I loved the metallic sky, the clammy wind that slapped our faces like some hurt and betrayed parent, the intersection that seemed to take forever to cross, and finally the fluorescent grail of the Twin Donut.

Why do I gravitate here? To old women with hands like yellowed lace clutching thick steaming cups? To this grudging-mother-love place that serves food with a lower-case "f"?

In this neighborhood, as in many others, I'm constantly imagining I see you out of the corner of my eye whenever there's a beggar or junkie just sitting on the sidewalk, propped up against a wall. Do you know what it's like to keep seeing you in my peripheral vision, wondering what I'll do if it's really you, then walking by relieved when it's not?

It's the defiant punk in me that wants to stay here, keeping one eye on the door. Yes, a Bavarian Kreme donut and coffee "to stay" seems like a punk gesture. Part of me thinks you'll be darkening the door any minute, come to whisk me back into that night, when we tried to focus on our images in the mirror as we rapidly undressed, charging hell-for-leather into our shared blind spot.

Unsatisfactory is the word to describe this piece of writing, that memory, our level of commitment to one another, and nothing seems to capture and express that better than this place. I think that Twin Donut should invent the Imperfect Love Donut, for the morning after.

Ladies Nite

is the time when
us gals can get ahead of
the wage imbalance
by having our
margaritas daiquiris longislandiceteas
for half price

the reduced price calculated
to get us twice as loopy,
to get us to show
what we least want to reveal
or at least lose track of our
train of thought (or his lies)
a giant step backward for our gender
but always good for business

Ladies nite!
all drinks $3.99!
and even watered-down peach and
barely banana
go right to our heads
after that pink-collar ghetto lunch
of Melba toast
petite salad and
soft-serve zero-percent-fat frozen yogurt

suddenly we're
spilling out into the street
bathed in the happy-hour orange

of the punch-clock sun
that's painting the tops of the buildings
kind of the way
this melon-colored buzz
pickles hope
and somehow we've made it
back home where we can
kick off our glass slippers
elevate our aching
feet

To Denise, My College Roommate

Somehow there was always hope
behind your dark, impenetrable thick walls —
countering your moods,
your unwashed hair,
were the wonderful
exotic almond eyes
the dimpled smile
that flashed out
like quick wit-lightning
or the eyes that slit into two narrow slices of chocolate pie
in answer to something
our dippy roommate said.

Mornings
I would walk into the bathroom down the hall
to the smell of Keri Lotion and Coast soap
as you and a friend from down the hall
cleaned off and talked,
washing sleep off both ways.

I should have your hope,
your bravery,
your bite-the-bullet surety
of things
right and wrong.
Your greatest gift to me
will be that whenever
I falter in my knowledge of things,
or in my decisions,
I will remember you.

Chemo

(for John)

Though we both had a sick sense
of humor,
it manifested itself in different ways.

You wore sincere baseball caps
to cover your baldness;
my way of coping would be
to buy a series of wigs,
each more artificial looking
than the last,
my fur-lined Dada heart
turned inside out
and worn on my head,
not my sleeve.

I guess that's the difference
between us.

Delivery Boys

I hear the buzzers,
the buzzers of all the women
in my building.
My buzzer will ring soon,
as we are each called upon by
our small and dark
or tall and swarthy dates.
Dates bearing food.
They are the best dates of all —
they bring the food
and then they leave.

Orion's Mother to Her Son

You began as a scatological gleam
in my eye.
When your father and I saw you
spray-painting epithets on the nursery walls
we knew you were destined for greatness
a chosen one for
kicking up people's shit
a human anvil for their complacency
you were all that and more
a threat to the spineless
a low-hanging branch
a tower of purposeful perversity
on your first grade report card
your teacher wrote:
"Plays hell with others."

But now you're on spoken word CD
anthologies
OK but that power ballad duet
you did with Axl Rose for Zima beer
was the last straw
you've gone soft
sold out and become a pussy-poet
like the gelatinous maraschino cherry
on a rubbery pudding.
Your pubic area
has the mange and
now the children play
in the antibacterial sandbox
of your gentrified asshole.

WORDS AND MUSIC

Song Request

Play "Kiss" by Prince:
I make this reasonable request at a
slick dance club that's inside a
suburban Florida strip mall.
Our friend Jackie
who lives in our parents' condo development
has dragged my brother Paul and me here
for a night of — what?

"We don't play progressive dance music," snaps the catty DJ.
I don't even know what that is.
So humiliating to be rejected in this backwater,
when I've danced at clubs in Detroit, New York and London.

Paul looks so different tonight, in the
black leather motorcycle jacket
Jackie talked him into buying at TJ Maxx yesterday.
He's smitten
but she's already trolling the floor
for older guys,
because they're more likely to own
a boat and other expensive things.

I don't care.
I just want to hear "Kiss,"
that impossibly funky tune
with Prince shrieking over a
deep bass groove.

Heartbreak and disappointment
are on tap tonight for this
brother and sister,
two fish out of water.

Listening to Sonny Rollins

Behind the champagne-colored curtain
at the Paradiso Café,
adulthood dwelt.
It waited like martini in the glass,
and the olive at the bottom
was masturbation
or period
or both.

We toasted our future,
Mom, Dad, my brother and I:
two glasses of white wine
clinking against
two kiddie cocktails —
embarrassingly bright pink liquid
garnished with plastic
monkey or mermaid perched
on the rim.

Behind that curtain
lay the promise of sophistication:
 dinner dresses
 cocktail rings
 jazz bands
a place to wear your finest.

I pulled the fabric aside once
after dinner
when I was eight or nine
stuffed with ravioli
and light-headed from my first sugary taste
of Asti Spumante.

There was nothing there
but a brick wall.

Love Poem

(after Emily Dickinson)

Love, what is love?
A shining grin from up above?
In other words — the Sun!

A Talisman of crimson felt
To signify where ardor dwelt
For a long vanished One?

Love can occur in Rain or Snow
Rare warmth to make the shivers go
And put Winter on the run.

Love is lips of pink and nails of red
Black satin where two lives are wed
And Families joined — dancing circles begun.

You can love a squirrel, a clown or a tree
The object matters not, if Love is given free
And excludes none.

To a Bass Player

My dad once had a stand-up bass
like yours;
it moldered in the basement for many years
before finally being sold.
It's probably somewhere in downtown Detroit now,
where Mom and Dad fear to tread,
being plied by youthful black fingers
dreaming of the city's rebirth
and a ticket out.

Dad once played there —
Polish weddings and big-band orchestras
and small ensembles —
on the one LP they made,
you can hear muted applause
between numbers.

But the city's changed since then;
my brother and I, raised in the suburbs,
could only dream of the city it was,
and a bus ticket back
to bygone cosmopolitan greatness.

Big-Time Sarah

We had cricks in our
necks
the next
day,
from bobbing our heads
all night
to the music.

Segregated to the back room
of that smoky bar,
we latecomers had to
wait
until people up front
left —
then we could move to
where
we could see Sarah
and her Chicago Blues Machine.

We didn't talk much,
just sat staring
at the scuffed wood table,
but when a really good
song
began rhythmically
grinding out
cigarette butts,
we'd bang our beer
steins,
too.

We could feel the beat
percolating through
the floorboards,
massaging our tired feet
through our
workaday pumps
and loafers
and sneakers.

Late in the set,
the band slipped easily into
"Miss You" by the Stones,
and in that cramped bar
we knew we were
witnessing a world we
could never enter:
memories of
freedom-fighting days
lurking in the crook
of the sax,
coiled tight
in her
vibrato.

The Ballad of Carla Faye Tucker

(to the tune of "Ol' Dan Tucker")

On death row for her attacks
Killed some folks with an old pickax
Later on said she found God
Folks in Texas just called her odd

Git out the way for Carla Faye Tucker
She's gonna git her last supper
Supper's over and Carla's cookin'
Victim's families just stand there lookin'

She's the darling of the press
Waltzin' around in a snow white dress
Decided to become born again
Just in time for her in-jec-tion

Git out the way for Carla Faye Tucker
She's gonna git her last supper
Supper's over and Carla's cookin'
Paparazzi just stand there lookin'

Baby killers and trailer trash
Crazy drivers with cars that crash
Governor says fry these ol' gals
save our taxes and clear the jails

Git out the way for Carla Faye Tucker
She's gonna git her last supper
Supper's over and Carla's cookin'
Hangin' judge just stands there lookin'

Cootie Love Doll

She's got cooties and she knows it. She says poem like "pwem." She's my high maintenance girl. She's got the blues 'cause the cooties her did choose. Bedbugs have a way of breedin', when your love comes a-knockin'. She fell for some cootie-ridden pal, but she's my high maintenance, hi-gloss gal. She left a trail of sorrow cause the cooties they did burrow and their electric glow in the night did give everyone a fright. And she reads by their light, a "pwem" she does recite. No one will touch her, she's a caste away, untouchable, unbroachable, unscalable, high maintenance, highly communicable doll. Off her pillow cooties roll. She is their beach, like that dirty joke with ants: one sleeps in the nostril, one sleeps in the bush, one sleeps in the asshole, all chased by different monsters in their dreams. Can she hear their screams? No, she's my high maintenance girl, flaked out with earbuds and a blindfold. She does a dance of cootie photosynthesis, I don't know what kind of sin this is, but whatever game she did play, she musta got her way. She uses bug Afro Sheen, she's my funky cootie queen. A virtual cootie machine.

Family

What is family?
free-floating DNA
combining & recombining
in random, surprising ways

You can't pick your family
but you can pick a spouse or a friend
this is nature's exit strategy
to achieve a happy end

Family is whomever you care for
my family members are loving but flawed
my mom watches Fox News
I watch PBS, CNN and The Daily Show
What can I say? We know what we know…

For a long time my brother struggled
with demons in his isolation
but now that he's turned 60
he's finally begun his adult education

My friends drive me crazy sometimes
their habits can be whack
but when push comes to shove
we know we've got each other's backs

And my husband, he's the best
a pro at mimicking Trump
makes me laugh so hard
I have to take a dump

Family, what is family?
random groups you shape and form —
heroes? saviors?
No, just comfy — like old shoes that are worn

Subway Beat

Two boys enter the subway car
with a boombox.
I watch them ride the poles, defy gravity.
Weightless youth somersaulting, swooping, hanging
to nasal sampled voices and swaggering drum machine.
It's not my thing but
I'm glad to hear modest applause when they finish,
a few coins dropped
in a passed baseball cap.
They exit next stop.
Still gripping a pole
as the train picks up speed and
leans into a curve,
I almost feel my own
feet lift.

The Amoeba Song

Tiny one-celled animal,
I'd like to adopt you for a pet
If I could only find you
In this vast universe

I'd sleep with you next to me on my pillow
(or maybe I already am)
But I would like to keep you
Where I can see you, tiny animal

O microscopic flagellate
You move so gracefully
Through time and space
You put the jellyfish to shame

CHORUS:

My own amoeba
I'd like to cuddle you
Make you a little suit and
Introduce you to other protozoa

Tiny flake of existence
So helpless weightless in my hand
I'd like to stroke your filaments
And watch you skate across the surface of my eye

You are so infinitesimal
You make me wonder
If anything I do really matters

It's paradoxical
How someone so small
Can make me ponder
The larger questions of life

Spring's First Bloom

New spring shoots
Curl and unfurl
Tentative buds
Coyly they show
Streams of petals
Cascading and kind
Damp scent swelling
To overflow
My senses so starved
For green, pink and yellow.

Soon they will bloom
Abundant as stars
Everywhere raising
Their eyes to the sun —
I want to pick one
As I turn my gaze
To a girl on the train
With teeming bouquets.

The Hearse for Evel Knievel

The hearse for Evel Knievel reached high, high to the sky and on its
back door in gold leaf were the words, “The Tall Guy”
for Evel jumped in death even as he did in life,
        jumped cactus-like, jumped canyon-like
        jumped stadium-like, jumped 18-wheeler-like,
        jumped I-don’t-want-to-mess-my-car-in-that-puddle-like,
        jumped candlestick-like, jumped haystack-like,
        jumped overpass-like, jumped Mideast Peace Talks-like,
        jumped chicken-crossing-the-road-like,
        jumped SWAT-team-like, jumped airport security-like,
        jumped Hull-Rust-Mahoning open pit ore mine-like,

and even now (in death as in life) he needed max headroom
and his wife said, “I missed my period last week, and I am happy.”
Jumped finally.

Pope-tastic

I wish they would open a Pope-tique in the concourse under Madison Square Garden so that I could buy some Pope-obilia from the Popefest for my Pope chest. I don't have a ticket for the Pope-ercade scheduled to process through Central Park, but I do think it's going to be Pope-tastic. If it's hot that day, I guess the crowd can cool off with Pope-sicles.

I was skeptical about the new Pope, but now I really like him. He's a disruptor, a boat-rocker and that is just what the Vatican needs, full as it is of wannabes and Pope-sers (poseurs). He's a refreshing cornuPopia of hope and change. And yet he remains true to himself and not beholden to the latest trends in Pope Culture.

I hope Francis isn't stalked too aggressively by the Pope-erazzi. It would be a shame if he had to go all medieval Pope on them. But I wouldn't want to be the inter-Poper, a party-Poper in that situation. Nope.

Resurrection

(for Sal Salasin)

I was having a perfectly pleasant
near-death experience
when some nincompoop with paddles
brought me back
will you please turn your hymnals
to page 336

Astonished to find
I was still working at my desk
even though
my heart had stopped
as unsubtly
as a senile person
in midsentence

I expire but
the OJ trial goes on
juicing on its own entropy
an endless procession
of new jurors
like the eager or terrified
at the gates of
Heaven or Hell

my eyes
I don't remember blinking
but according to the experts
they've been closed
for some time

Crown Industries,
Manufacturers of roll-up
plastic lighted portable disco dance floors
and other essential products for home and
industry
is proud to sponsor
the Loebner Prize for Artificial Intelligence

I try to stay awake
until I realize I am unconscious
drifting through the galaxy
picking my way among the celestial bodies —
But this is how I always pictured death!
How dumb!

And I startle myself, once again, awake.
Does this qualify as prayer? I don't know.
It was just an observation.

Life Café Shuffle

cash register doing perpetual motion calculator can-can/
facetious impostors of the Lost Generation pantomime debate/
pulsating House from passing car blots out Mr. Softee theme/
shrunken homunculoid cab drivers stretch to hang scrawny arms
out taxi windows/ Madonna gardens mediate hallucinatory
visitations/ a convenient bush of recyclable plastic milk jugs
sways like kinetic sculpture/ rat the size of medium gray squirrel
strolls politely alongside then ducks into empty tenement/ turn
my deaf ear to stupid street corner pussy calls/ that deaf ear
serves me well/ O rats O cats O homunculi O steamy Life Café
veggie chili

The 23rd Psalm for Brunettes

Audrey Hepburn is my Shepherd; I shall not bleach.
She maketh me to lay my head down in the ebony sink:
She leadeth me beside the auburn rinse.
She restoreth my natural chestnut tint:
She massageth my scalp for my follicles' sake.
Yea, though I walk through the shadow of leggy Valley blondes,
I will fear no peroxide:
For thou art with me;
Thy conditioner and thy blow dryer, they comfort me.
Thou preparest a day spa before me in the presence of
dumb guys at bars who ignorest me because I wearest glasses
and lackest flaxen locks;
Thou annointest my head with Clairol Herbal Essences; My cap
runneth over.
Shirley Temple and Charo shall follow me all the days of my life,
but they shall not catch me,
and I will dwell in the House of the Cher forever.

"Boot Eating Scooter Trash"

— band name posted at Restaurant Florent

We're boot eating scooter trash
we're raising dust bunnies in the backyard
we leave sugar for the ants
let's fuck in my hutch

We're boot eating scooter trash
we got burlap sheets
our dogs know how to scratch
   in all the wrong places
let's rut in my rutted dirt driveway

We're boot eating scooter trash
for company we break out
   the Spam, Bud, and pork & beans
we leave our children with the Board of Ed
coast is clear — let's do it
   under the sticky No Pest Strip in the garage

We're boot eating scooter trash
we cleaned up a little
swept the soil into neat piles
and hosed down the aluminum siding
let's skinny dip in my above-the-ground pool
   with the skin of scum on top
and sink down to the bottom
and grind 'til the silt
lodges permanently in our cracks

Epiphany

The choir director says
they are "voicing" the organ
in the church next door —
pricking the bottom of each huge
pipe to give it a certain sound.
Hence the temporary practice room we are presently in.
I glance at a black and white photo
on the wall
of a soup kitchen line —
fallen angels
waiting in the snow.
My eyes linger on the scene
hoping some compassion will seep in.
It doesn't.
This fluorescent-lit
catechetical hell is not
conducive to harmony or generosity —
folding chairs cramped together,
short in the portable keyboard
that robs notes.

A week later, we're still in this dubious
practice space
but this time I notice
strange posters for the Episcopal Church
in the hallway.
One is a reproduction of that
famous painting of St. Sebastian
being pierced by arrows.

Underneath it says,
"If you think practicing your faith
is inconvenient now, you should
have seen it in his day."
Another depicts miserable souls
stewing in the netherworld
with the caption,
"Contrary to popular thinking,
stress is not a twentieth-century phenomenon."
Walking home that night, I finally get it:
not much has changed
through the centuries…

About the Author

Carol Wierzbicki's work has been published in *Long Shot*, *Public Illumination*, *Evergreen Review, Big Bridge*, *Many Mountains Moving*, *The Otter*, and *The Bug Book* (Poets Wear Prada). Her chapbook is *Top Teen Greatest Hits* (Poets Wear Prada, 2009 and 2017). She is writing two fiction books for children.